Ilia Chavchavadze

THE HERMIT

A LEGEND

THE HERMIT

A LEGEND

Ilia Chavchavadze

Translated from the Georgian by Marjory S. Wardrop

Edited by Jack Monro

Illustrations © Glagoslav Publications 2025

Introduction © Glagoslav Publications 2025

Translator's Biography © Glagoslav Publications 2025

www.glagoslav.com

ISBN: 978-1-80484-234-8

This book is in copyright. No part of this publication may be reproduced, stored in a retrieval system or transmitted in any form or by any means without the prior permission in writing of the publisher, nor be otherwise circulated in any form of binding or cover other than that in which it is published without a similar condition, including this condition, being imposed on the subsequent purchaser.

Ilia Chavchavadze

The HERMIT

A LEGEND

GLAGOSLAV CLASSICS

CONTENTS

Introduction 7

Preface 17
The Hermit 21

Ilia Chavchavadze:
Architect of a Nation's Soul 51
Marjory Scott Wardrop:
The Indispensable Intermediary 60

INTRODUCTION

It's a peculiar magic, isn't it, the way certain texts can lie dormant, nestled within the vast, echoing archives of literature, only to be rediscovered and find fresh resonance with a new generation? One might stumble upon them in a dusty corner of a forgotten library shelf, or perhaps, as is increasingly the case in our digital age, through a serendipitous click, a footnote in an academic paper, or a recommendation whispered across continents via the ether. And when such a text is prised open, it's like uncovering a time capsule, not just of words and stories, but of an entire epoch's sensibility, its anxieties, its aspirations. Such is the case with Ilia Chavchavadze's poetic narrative, *The Hermit*, brought to the English-speaking world in 1895 through the remarkable dedication of Marjory Scott Wardrop.

Here we are, in 2025, holding a work that first breathed in Georgian, a language of ancient lineage and unique beauty, in the latter half of the 19th century, then found an English voice just as Victoria's long reign was drawing to its close. To approach *The Hermit* today is to engage in a multi-layered act of literary archaeology. We are not merely reading a poem; we are peering through a series of lenses: Chavchavadze's original vision, steeped in Georgian Orthodoxy, folklore, and a burgeoning national consciousness; Wardrop's Victorian interpretation, filtered through her own era's understanding of faith, romance, and the "exotic" East; and finally, our own contemporary perspective, shaped by a world Chavchavadze could scarcely have imagined, yet one that still grapples with the very questions he poses.

Before we delve into the spectral, haunting beauty of *The Hermit* itself, it is paramount, indeed essential, to understand the colossal figure of its author. Ilia Chavchavadze (1837-1907) is not merely a Georgian writer; he is, without hyperbole, the cornerstone of modern Georgian identity, often referred to as the "Father of the Nation." To Georgians, he is what Shakespeare is to the English, Goethe to the Germans, or Pushkin to the Russians – and then some. His influence transcends literature, permeating politics, education, social reform, and even banking (he founded the first successful commercial bank in Georgia, aiming to support the Georgian peasantry and nobility against Russian economic dominance).

Imagine Georgia in the 19th century: a proud, ancient kingdom, with a history stretching back millennia, swallowed by the insatiable appetite of the Russian Empire. Its language was suppressed in schools and official institutions, its unique culture under threat of Russification, its aristocracy often lured by the glamour and opportunities of St. Petersburg, sometimes at the expense of their native land. Into this challenging milieu stepped Chavchavadze, a nobleman by birth but a radical intellectual by inclination. He saw his nation teetering on the brink of cultural oblivion and dedicated his life, his formidable intellect, and his considerable talents to its revival. He wrote poetry, novels, essays, and journalistic pieces, all with the fiery purpose of awakening a national spirit, of reminding Georgians of their rich heritage, and of charting a path towards a modern, enlightened future, yet one firmly rooted in Georgian traditions. His rallying cry was, famously, "Language, Homeland, Faith" – a tripartite foundation upon which he believed Georgian identity could be rebuilt and sustained.

Chavchavadze's contemporaries, figures like Akaki Tsereteli, another titan of Georgian literature, and Vazha-Pshavela, the poet of the mountains whose work explored the profound relationship between humanity and nature, formed a constellation of talent known as the Tergdaleulebi – "those who drank the waters of the Terek." This referred to the young Georgian intellectuals who, having studied in Russian universities (crossing the Terek River in the Caucasus mountains to get there), returned to Georgia imbued with European Enlightenment ideals and a burning desire to apply them to their homeland's specific needs. They were modernisers, but also passionate patriots. Chavchavadze was their undisputed leader, his journal Iveria becoming the principal mouthpiece for this national renaissance.

His life was one of relentless activity and profound courage. He championed literacy, advocated for land reform, fought against serfdom (which was abolished later in Georgia than in Russia proper), and tirelessly worked to preserve the Georgian language and the autocephaly (independence) of the Georgian Orthodox Church. It is a testament to his impact, and perhaps an indictment of the forces he opposed, that his life was cut tragically short. In 1907, Ilia Chavchavadze was assassinated, a murder that sent shockwaves through Georgia and is still debated and mourned. His death cemented his status as a national martyr, and he was later canonised as Saint Ilia the Righteous by the Georgian Orthodox Church.

So, when we pick up *The Hermit* (განდეგილი, Gandegili), first published in 1883, we are not reading a mere flight of romantic fancy, though it possesses an ethereal, almost sublime quality. We are engaging with a work produced by a man deeply immersed in the socio-political and spiritual struggles of his time. The poem tells the story of a monk who retreats to a remote, ice-bound cave high in the Caucasus mountains, seeking spiritual purity and communion with God through extreme asceticism.

He renounces the world, its temptations, its vanities, believing that in splendid isolation, amidst the raw, unforgiving majesty of nature, he can achieve a state of grace. His life is one of prayer, fasting, and contemplation, his only companions the eagles and the eternal snows.

But, as is often the case in such narratives of extreme renunciation, the world, in its most alluring and perhaps most innocent form, finds a way to intrude. A shepherdess, lost in a storm, stumbles upon his hermitage. Her youth, her beauty, her vulnerability, and her simple, unadorned faith challenge the hermit's carefully constructed spiritual fortress. He is faced with a profound crisis: does true holiness lie in solitary withdrawal, or in compassionate engagement with the suffering and beauty of humanity? Is God found only in the silent peaks, or also in the warmth of a human heart, in the plea of a fellow soul?

Chavchavadze, himself a devout Christian but also a pragmatic reformer, uses this seemingly simple narrative to explore complex theological and philosophical questions. Is the hermit's path an act of supreme devotion, or a form of spiritual pride, a subtle rejection of God's creation in its human form? The poem doesn't offer easy answers. Instead, it immerses the reader in the hermit's internal turmoil, the grandeur of the mountain landscape mirroring the vastness of his spiritual quest and the starkness of his dilemma. There are echoes here, perhaps, of the Desert Fathers, of Tennyson's "St. Simeon Stylites," or even of Milton's depiction of Christ's temptation in the wilderness in Paradise Regained. Yet, Chavchavadze's treatment is uniquely Georgian, imbued with the specific spirituality of the Caucasus and the deep connection to landscape that permeates Georgian culture.

The poem can also be read, allegorically, as a commentary on Georgia itself. Could the hermit's isolation, his turning away from the world, be a metaphor for a nation retreating into itself, risking stagnation or irrelevance? Or, conversely, is it a call to preserve a core spiritual integrity against the overwhelming pressures of external forces (like Russification)? Chavchavadze, the great public figure, the tireless nation-builder, writing about a man who utterly rejects society, presents a fascinating paradox. Perhaps he understood, better than most, the allure of solitude and the spiritual nourishment it can offer, even as he dedicated his own life to the very public, often messy, business of national revival. Or perhaps he was issuing a subtle warning against an inward-looking piety that neglects the pressing needs of the community.

Now, let us turn to the remarkable woman who brought this poem to us: Marjory Scott Wardrop (1869-1909). Her story is, in its own way, as compelling as Chavchavadze's. Born into a comfortable middle-class family in Chislehurst, Kent, Marjory developed an early and passionate interest in languages and foreign cultures. It was her brother, Oliver Wardrop, later a distinguished diplomat and the first British Chief Commissioner of Transcaucasia in Georgia (1919-1921), who first introduced her to the Georgian language. What began as a scholarly pursuit soon blossomed into a profound love affair with Georgia – its history, its literature, its people.

At a time when opportunities for women in academia and international affairs were severely limited, Marjory Wardrop became one of the foremost Western Kartvelologists (scholars of Georgian studies) of her day. She taught herself Georgian – no mean feat, given its unique script and complex grammar, and the scarcity of learning resources in Britain at the time. She travelled to Georgia in 1894-95 (a daring undertaking for a lone woman, though often accompanied by her brother) and again in 1896, immersing herself in the culture, befriending key intellectual figures (including, one presumes, those who knew Chavchavadze well, though Chavchavadze himself was still very much alive and active during her visits), and collecting manuscripts.

Her translation of *The Hermit*, published in 1895 by Bernard Quaritch in London, was a landmark. It was one of the very first major works of Georgian literature to appear in English, rendered with a sensitivity and poetic grace that speaks volumes of her linguistic skill and her deep understanding of the original text's spirit. She followed this with other crucial translations, most notably her prose translation of Shota Rustaveli's 12th-century epic, The Knight in the Panther's Skin (ვეფხისტყაოსანი, Vepkhistqaosani), a monumental work that remains the cornerstone of Georgian secular literature. She worked on this tirelessly for years, and it was published posthumously, lovingly edited by her brother Oliver, in 1912.

Reading Wardrop's 1895 translation today, we must, of course, acknowledge the passage of time. Her English is undeniably Victorian, with a certain formality and poetic diction characteristic of the era. Some modern readers might find it a touch archaic. Yet, there is a distinct charm and a palpable integrity to her work. She clearly strove for fidelity not just to the letter but to the spirit of Chavchavadze's poem, capturing its solemn beauty, its romantic grandeur, and its underlying spiritual intensity. One can sense her profound respect for the original and her earnest desire to share its treasures with an English-speaking audience largely ignorant of Georgia's rich literary tradition. Her work was truly pioneering, building a bridge between two vastly different cultures. The Wardrop Collection of Georgian books and manuscripts, bequeathed by Sir Oliver Wardrop to the Bodleian Library at Oxford, remains a vital resource for scholars to this day, a testament to the siblings' shared passion. Tragically, like Chavchavadze, Marjory Wardrop also died relatively young, at the age of forty, her immense contribution to Georgian studies cut short.

So, why should we, in 2025, return to *The Hermit*? In our hyper-connected, often secular, and relentlessly noisy world, the figure of the hermit, seeking silence and transcendence, holds a peculiar fascination. Chavchavadze's poem explores timeless questions that continue to resonate: What is the nature of true faith? Where is God to be found – in splendid isolation or in the messy, compassionate embrace of humanity? What is the relationship between the individual spiritual quest and the needs of the community? How do we balance contemplation and action, renunciation and engagement?

Furthermore, in an age increasingly aware of environmental fragility, the poem's vivid depiction of the awesome, indifferent power of the Caucasus mountains speaks with renewed force. The hermit's intimate, albeit austere, relationship with the natural world offers a counterpoint to our often exploitative and destructive tendencies.

Reading *The Hermit* today is also an act of cultural empathy and historical recovery. It allows us a precious glimpse into the soul of 19th-century Georgia, a nation striving to preserve its identity against formidable odds, through the eyes of its most revered national poet. And it allows us to appreciate the extraordinary dedication of a Victorian woman, Marjory Wardrop, who, driven by intellectual curiosity and a deep affection for a distant land, laboured to bring its literary gems to light.

This edition, then, presents Wardrop's 1895 translation as a historical document in its own right, a testament to a particular moment in the cross-cultural exchange between Georgia and the West. Whilst a modern translator might choose different diction, a different cadence, there is an undeniable power in experiencing Chavchavadze's vision through the lens of one of its earliest and most devoted English interpreters.

Prepare, therefore, to be transported to the snow-capped peaks of the Caucasus, to enter the chill, sacred space of the hermit's cell, and to witness a profound drama of the human spirit unfold. Ilia Chavchavadze's *The Hermit*, in Marjory Wardrop's translation, is more than just a poem; it is an invitation to reflect on the enduring questions of existence, framed by a landscape of breathtaking majesty and a historical context of profound national significance. It is a work that, despite its age and the cultural distances it traverses, still has much to say to us, if only we take the time to listen.

PREFACE

While most English readers are, to some extent, acquainted with the literature of Persia, few are aware that Georgian literature exists. Yet, Georgia is well worthy of attention. *The Man in the Panther's Skin* by Shota Rustaveli, the great epic poet of the 12th century, loses nothing by comparison with Ferdowsi's *Shahnameh*. But what modern Persian can be placed beside Nikoloz Baratashvili or Ilia Chavchavadze?

Endowed by nature with exceptional gifts and assimilating the cultures of both East and West, the Christian kingdom of the Caucasus achieved a high degree of refinement and enlightenment at a very early date. Despite the fierce blasts of war that have swept ceaselessly over the land, the light of literature has been kept alive.

Prince Ilia Chavchavadze was born in 1837. His family produced many remarkable figures, including the poet Prince Alexander Chavchavadze (1786–1846), who was greatly influenced by the writings of Lord Byron. Prince Ilia received his education at the Tbilisi Gymnasium and the University of St. Petersburg.

In 1863, he founded the journal *Sakartvelos Moambe*, which had a profound influence on his countrymen. In the same year, he wrote his novella, *Is That a Man?*, which depicted the aimless life of the average country squire. This tale raised a storm of ill will, but it achieved its author's object: the landed gentry saw their faults mercilessly mirrored. First, they were angry, then ashamed, and finally awakened to self-improvement.

Chavchavadze's literary activity extends over nearly forty years and falls into three phases. In the first, he is critical and satirical, endeavoring to rouse people from their lethargy. In the second, he encourages them to lead a nobler life by reminding them of their country's glorious past and depicting the heroic deeds of patriots. Finally, he entered a phase that may be described as almost purely aesthetic.

To this last division belongs *The Hermit*, written in 1883. Based on a legend, the poem also has, in my opinion, a symbolic meaning. Is the hermit not meant to represent medievalism, and the shepherd girl—so bewitching and bright—the Renaissance, which came so much later to Georgia than to the West? Before her beauty and gladness, the old life cannot be lived; it must either share in her joy or die.

From ancient Buddhist legends to modern French romances, many stories have been written on the temptation of holy recluses. *The Hermit* differs from them all in its wonderful simplicity.

Here, we have no theatrical machinery, no dazzling wealth, no dreams of power to tempt the monk from his solitude, poverty, and suffering. There is no vision of Cleopatra or Semiramis to beguile him from the path of duty, but only a simple maiden, innocent and lovely, who tells him of the pure loves of mankind and the joyousness of life. Yet, we feel that the temptation is all the more subtle and strong for its very simplicity. In the original, the style is dignified and harmonious, and the descriptions are full of poetry and a tender sympathy with nature in all her moods.

Prince Ilia is distinguished not only as a poet and novelist. He was the editor of the daily paper *Iveria*, published in Tbilisi, and the managing director of the Land Bank of the Nobility—an institution that devoted all its profits to educational and philanthropic work. He was also an eloquent orator and the most prominent figure in the nation's social life.

I regret that my translation does so little justice to the original. The difficulty of learning a tongue hitherto unknown in the West, and of rendering an idiom unallied to any known family of languages, may be pleaded as some excuse for my shortcomings.

Marjory Wardrop
Kertch, Crimea,
October 1895

THE HERMIT

I

There, where Mount Kazbek rears his noble brow.
   Where eagle cannot soar, nor vulture fly,
Where, never melted by the sun's warm rays,
   The frozen rain and snow eternal lie;
Far from the world's wild uproar set apart,
   There, in the awful solitude and calm,
Where thunder's mighty roar rules o'er these realms,
   Where frost doth dwell and winds sing forth their
        psalm;
There stood, in former days, a house of God,
   Built by devout and holy men, the fame
Of that old temple still the folk hold dear.
   And Bethlehem is still, to-day, its name.
The ice-bound wall of that secluded shrine
   Was hollowed out from craggy, massive block,
And, like an eagle's eyrie on the cliff,
   The door stood carved in the solid rock.
Straight downward from this gate unto the path
   There hung descending a rough iron chain,
And save by that strange ladder's aid alone
   Man could in no wise thereto entrance gain.

II

In days of old, monks left this world of woe,
  And there they dwelt, devoted unto God,
In that wild wilderness they sang their songs
  Of praise, and in the path of saints they trod.
There they withdrew to seek God's solitude,
  There they abandoned all earth's vanity,
And, in that everlasting dwelling, sought
  To fit themselves for God's eternity.
Those holy fathers sacrificed this world,
  And, for the pain they suffered in that shrine,
The mountaineers revered them, and they sang
  The praise of good deeds, and of grace divine.
And by the people still that place is held
  So holy, even now, that in the chase
A refuge there the wounded beast may seek,
  For there no huntsman dares to leave his trace;
None save the man whose life is given to God
  Can rest within that ruin's sacred shade.
And he who breaks this law must perish there
  By swift, avenging lightning's trenchant blade.

III

And there, in yon forsaken hermitage.
  An anchorite took up his lone abode,
He left the fleeting world and, set apart,
  Gave up the present for the life with God.
Far from the dwelling of the sinful man,
  Far from the realm where wickedness holds sway,
Where e'en the just man scarcely can escape
  From Satan's tempting power; where, night and day,
Man is pursued by evil, like a thief
  Which tries to seize upon him unaware;
Where, e'en if right be known by its true name,
  The hand of sin will still all evil dare;
Where faithlessness, corruption, rapine dwell,
  And brother for his brother's blood doth lust,
Where discord turns the purest love of friends,
  By scandal's breath, to hatred and mistrust . . .
He left that fleeting world where every gift
  Is as a snare, and beauty but a lure;
The devil uses even virtues there
  To wile th'unwary, and his prey secure.

IV

Alone the hermit dwelt, amid this ice,
   A solitary anchorite, his mind
He troubled not henceforth with painful thoughts
   Of all the sinful cares of human kind.
He banished from his heart each worldly grief,
   Each thought, concern and wish that was profane.
That he might stand before the judgment seat
   Of God, with spirit pure and free from stain.
Both day and night, with lamentation, prayer,
   And scourging martyred he, for his soul's sake,
His flesh, and, like a vessel washfid clean,
   With tears he strove his spirit pure to make;
Both day and night, with sighing and complaint,
   The icy rocks re-echoed forth his groans,
And his fast-flowing, suppliant tears ceased not
   In that lone home of weeping and of moans.
Far from this transitory earth apart.
   His spirit like a flowfir there did bloom;
Each worldly wish was calmed and laid to rest.
   And all desire was buried in the tomb.

V

He was not old—upon his saint-like face
   His soul's nobility was pictured fair,
It could be seen his spirit was the home
   Of other thoughts than those of worldly care.
His features melancholy, thin and sad,
   Yet beamed with loveliness of grace divine,
Which from his deeply wrinkled, lofty brow,
   Like bright encircling halo, forth did shine.
So gentle and so sweet was the deep thought
   Expressed in his clear, meditative eyes,
It seemed as if in them was mirrored forth
   Virtue herself, arrayed in modest guise;
As if, with gentle gladness, they rejoiced
   At Paradise's open entrance gate,
Together with his soul, to meet their Lord,
   And hastened on, with faith secure, elate.
In fasting and in prayer, with body weak,
   He lived like holy martyrs who attain,
By many roads of suffering and of woe.
   To glory, conquering heroes over pain.

VI

His witness was accepted of the Lord,
  Who hearkened to his humble servant's sighs
And, as a token of His grace, vouchsafed
  A miracle in answer to his cries.
In the dark cell wherein the monk did pray
  The window faced the dawning day's first gleam,
And downward, in a flood of lustrous light,
  The rays of sun and moon did through it stream.
And o'er yon solitary mountain peak
  When rose the sun's glad rays of morning light,
Through that small window in his lonely cell
  The beam shone down, a column broad and bright.
Lo ! when the hermit prayed, it was ordained
  That on the ray his book of prayers should stand.
And on that solid sunbeam did it rest
  Secure and safe, by God's divine command . . .
Thus passed his days, and thus rolled on the years,
  And, as a sign that God approved the way
Wirerein he walked, thus pure and without sin,
  This wonder was performed day by day.

VII

One evening, from long vigils weary, worn,
   Forth through the door he dragged his limbs, and fixed
His meditative gaze upon the plain
   Stretched, verdant-carpeted, the hills betwixt.
And round the peak, like fan of flaming fire,
   The heav'ns with a broad-stretching glory gleamed.
Like to a brazier, burned the bright blue sky.
   And sparks of yellow, and deep crimson-hued.
Glittered among the clouds; bent back by them,
   They trembled with a thousand tints imbued.
The hermit was entranced, and raptured gazed—
   So wondrous fair, so glorious was the sight—
Upon the splendour of the glowing sun
   As on a living picture of God's might . . .
But suddenly the wind arose; o'er rocks.
   Ravines and caverns blew the stormy blast,
And, like a serpent, over Kazbek's peak
   A darkly low'ring cloud, swift gliding, passed.

VIII

It crept along, tyrannical, immense,
  And stretched across the heav'ns' expansive vault,
Then burst the thunderclap, and roared with rage,
  As one who doth his deadly foe assault.
The heaven and earth were straight with trembling seized
  At that loud noise, that terrible uproar—
Then sudden darkness overspread the sky.
  And hissing hail forth from the clouds did pour.
Upon the earth, all intermingled, burst,
  With furious din, the thunder, lightning, hail,
The raging wind blew fiercely 'mong the rocks,
  With angry whirl, a wild, strong, howling gale;
All these together strove, so that it seemed
  As if God oped his vials of wrath, and hurled
An awful judgment down from heaven that day
  As retribution on His erring world . . .
But now the monk took refuge in his cell,
  He prayed, with fervently upraised hand,
Before the Virgin's image, that the Lord
  From sin and ruin would redeem the land.

IX

Then suddenly, he heard a human voice,
  And, startled at this unaccustomed sound,
Again he listened, and he heard beneath
  As if one called from out the mirk profound.
Quickly unto the door the hermit ran,
  Against the ladder saw a bending form.
And lo! a childish voice cried out aloud
  And begged a shelt'ring roof in that wild storm.
Say, can it be a son of man who roams
  In this fierce deluge, on this awesome night?
The wild beasts e'en lie cow'ring in their lairs,
  In fear they flee the fury of God's sight!
"Who art thou?" said the monk, "Art thou a man?
  "Or evil sprite sent by the devil here?"
"Human am I—I pray thee shelter me!
  "For God's love, save me now from death's dire fear!
"Dost thou not see that heaven is well-nigh rent
  "And, overwhelming, on the earth doth press?
"Is this a time for words! Oh, pity me!
  "Refuse me not a refuge in distress I"

X

"Thou sayest well. If thou be son of man
   "'Twere sin to leave thee to the storm a prey;
"If thou be spirit ill, then God must wish
   "To make a trial of His poor monk this day.
"Come up whoe'er thou art! God's will be done!
   "Hold fast this iron chain, and have no fear,
"It is a ladder safe, footholds there are
   "By which a man can mount securely here!"
At last he reached the monastery door,
   Climbing the steep ascent of that rough chain.
The hermit met him . . . "What or who is this?'
   In the deep gloom he asked himself in vain.
"Come in, whoe'er thou art, I'll shelter thee,
   "Let us communion take, kneel down and pray,"
This is my cell, and lo I it is God's house;
   "Here many a knee hath bent before this day."
He led the way; into the cell they came;
   Here was the darkness deeper, e'en despite
The ashes of the almost burnt-out fire
   Which in the gloom gleamed with a feeble light.

XI

Now, when God's Mother let this new-come guest
   Into the cell, and showed of wrath no sign,
The monk said in his heart: "'Tis son of man,
   "And not a spirit harmful and malign!"
The stranger sank down quickly, numbed and wet,
   And stirred the cinders, then recumbent lay
Upon the hearth, with both cold hands outstretched,
   Oyer the dying embers' fading ray.
"How cold it is! " exclaimed the shiv'ring guest,
   "Ugh! Ugh! I'm almost frozen into stone! "
The hermit started at the sound, 'twas like
   A maiden's voice, he trembled at her moan.
Could it then be that fate had hither sent
   This shape in woman's guise to be a test!
And, like a flash of lightning, came this thought
   Into the horror-stricken hermit's breast.
But e'en if fate had sent this for a trial.
   It must have been by God's own self designed;
Therefore he took it from the Lord in faith.
   In confidence and peace of heart resigned.

XII

"Hast thou no firewood?" asked the visitor,
  "Go, bring some here and light a fire! A load
"Upon my back, to-morrow, will I fetch;
  "But let me warm myself, for love of God!"
The hermit, from the corner, brought some wood
  To light the fire anew; the blaze that beamed
When it was kindled, fast dispersed the gloom,
  And through the darksome cell it brightly streamed.
But when the ray, cast from the lighted fire,
  Upon the stranger guest, there seated, glowed,
A picture of enchanting loveliness
  Unto the hermit's wond'ring eyes it showed.
Full of bewitching beauty, full of life,
  A youthful maiden by the fire reclined.
Of noble mien, yet meek, she seemed; her neck
  Was bare, and graceful as the timid hind.
The beauty shed abroad from her black eyes
  Disputed with the warmth cast by the glow
Of firelight, and beneath that conquering gaze
  It yielded up to her, and flickered low.

XIII

The grace of Love herself, if she desired
  To picture forth the beauties of her mind.
And if she dwelt incarnate on the earth,
  A fairer semblance could not wish to find.
One could not say if grace adorned her form
  Or if her form was ornament to grace;
E'en envy, hatred's self, could naught descry—
  In that fair maid, of fault there was no trace.
Who would not tremble fore her glorious eyes,
  Her brilliant cheeks, and bosom heaving high?
Look at her lips!.. It seems that Love has left
  A kiss imprinted on them tenderly ...
Who is not drawn and captivated held
  By mighty Beauty's all-enchanting power? ...
'Tis said that by its influence subdued
  The savage beasts are tamed, and gentle cower.
And e'en that hermit stem, severe and sad,
  Grew gentler and more mild, by beauty swayed;
With sorrow in his guileless heart, he gazed,
  His eye held captive by the lovely maid.

XIV

At length he asked her : "Who art thou, my child?
"What can have brought thee to this desert drear,
"In this rough weather, when the tempest wild
"Has almost flooded earth, afar and near?"
"A shepherd lass am I... Down in the lap
"Of Kazbek's mount my father's flocks I fed;
"Deceived were the sheep by the fresh grass,
"I followed them, and on they still were led.
"Fair was the evening, when the setting sun
"Was glowing, and upon the sky I gazed
"Until I could see naught but heaven's vault,
"For in its brilliant light my eyes were dazed.
"The great sun shone, surrounded with bright rays,
"Behind the mountain peak, and heart and eye
"Were ravished with the beauty of the sight—
"'Twas like God's face that beamed so fair on high.
"I quite forgot to heed my father's words :
"'My child, trust ne'er yon mountain, for I've seen
"'The stormy blast sweep suddenly from heav'n,
"'Although the sun rose glorious and serene.'

XV

"'It matters naught! Come,' said my eager heart,
  "'Dost thou not wish this wondrous scene to view?'
"Intent I gazed . . . but Kazbek suddenly "
  "Frowned fierce, and clouds o'erspread the heavens' blue.
"In one brief moment all was darkness drear,
  "And from the mountain blew a chilly wind.
"I wish'd to take the sheep home e'er nightfall,
  "But 'twas too late, the way I could not find.
"For suddenly the storm came sweeping on,
  "Like drops of lead the hail began to shower;
"I trembled for the sheep, but could do naught—
  "In that deep gloom fear robbed me of all power.
"Indeed this mountain treacherous is, and false;
  "For sudden darkness had obscured the day,
"The smiling heaven had changed to sudden hell,
  "And all my joy was turned into dismay.
"Ah! why did I not heed my father's words!
  "What will befall me! Woe is me! . . . They say,
I've heard it oft, that those who disobey
  "Their father ne'er can prosper in their way.

XVI

"I, disobedient to my father's words,
    "Had lost the sheep. I only was to blame.
"But (canst thou tell me?) how can one avoid
    "The law that fate inex'rable doth frame?
"It was not for the flocks I grieved alone,
    "Twas that my father dear would be alarmed—
"I am his only child, he loves me much—
    "Ah! sorely would he grieve if I were harmed.
"The sheep were gone—they were his sole support,"
    "His only means of livelihood and gain—
"Yet, were I only safe at home once more
    "He would not frown, lest he should cause me pain.
"I stood in that wild storm on yon hillside;
    "Upon the land, from heaven, the deluge poured,
"The mountain shook and trembled to its base
    "Beneath my feet, while loud the thunder roared.—
"What could I do! Where could I hope to find"
    "A shelter from the tempest's raging blast?
"Shall I be bold, and strive to reach my home,
    "Or trust to fate until the storm be past?

XVII

"But if I stay—who knows if I am safe
  "From this dark night's impending, awful doom!
"If I go forth—in some deep, rocky glen
  "I may be dashed to pieces in the gloom . . .
"Yet I resolved to take the homeward path;
  "And said : Whatever comes to pass is good! . . .
"Nor canst thou say that I mistook my way,"
  "For here in safety presently I stood.
"I felt the chain, and then I knew that this
  "Must be Mount Kazbek's far-famed, saintly shrine;
"Full often had I from my father heard
  "That here a monk lived for the life divine.
"With joy I called aloud, and called again;
  "My voice was powerless 'gainst the raging wind.
"'Woe unto me,' I cried, ' if none can hear,
  "'If on this night no shelter I shall find!'
"But God had mercy on me, and at last
  "My cry He carried through the storm to thee—
"I need not tell thee more—thou know'st the rest—
  "May God save thee, e'en as thou hast saved me."

XVIII

"Thanks are not due to me that thou art safe,
   "For God alone can save the child He made;
"He ever stretches forth a helping hand
   "That He may all His chosen creatures aid ..."
"It seems thou thoughtest me a spirit ill!"
   "Be not amazed nor troubled in thy mind.
"What being in the world would visit me,
   "A lonely monk forgotten by mankind!
"Hast thou no ties upon the earth, no friend,
   "No brother, sister, kin dear to thy heart?"
"These had I once; to all I said farewell.
   "To serve the Lord, from yon world did I part."
"Hast thou lived here for long? " "I cannot tell."
   "Thou canst not tell! " " My child, from all the fears
"Of yon fast-fleeting world apart I dwell.
   "What reck I of the flight of passing years?
"And dost thou live without a human friend?"
   "To me God's holy will was thus revealed."
"But why should God desire that man should stay
   "Alone amid these icy rocks concealed?

XIX

"May God not be displeased, nor thou, O monk!
  "For I am very ignorant in speech . . .
"When in yon vale below I watched my flocks,
  "And looked up here, as far as sight could reach,
"I often pondered o'er my father's words:
  "'That there a monk dwelt, in those realms of ice,
"'Who for his soul's sake suffered solitude,
  "'And of his body made a sacrifice.'
"This tale surprised me, for I could not think
  "How this should be a pleasing deed to God;
"He surely could not be displeased that man
  "Should love the world where He Himself had trod!
"I said within myself: 'How can this be?
  "'Why did God deck the earth and make it fair
"'If man should look upon it as a curse,
  "'And leave the world and all its beauties rare?
"'Should I abandon all, all earthly ties?
  "'From all my friends, and home, should I depart?
"'O God, forgive me! 'tis too hard a task!
  "'I could not with such ease crush my poor heart!'

XX

"How canst thou bear to leave the world of joy?
 "Its pleasures sweet thou surely knowest well!
"Death sways all here, but there is gladsome life:
 "Here grief abides, but there delight doth dwell.
"Hast thou from thy crushed heart torn ev'ry tie?
 "Does love no longer linger in thy breast?
"Hast thou not brought grief hither with thee too?
 "Do care and sorrow ne'er disturb thy rest?
"Do dreams of home ne'er haunt the weary hours?
 "Dost thou ne'er for thy friends and parents pine?
"Was there no heart to make thee happy there—
 "No heart which throbbed in harmony with thine?
'How couldst thou leave all love? ..." "Hear me, my child!
 "The soul is dearer than all vain delight;
"It is a captive in yon fleeting world,
 "These joys are chains that stay its upward flight."
"Are all who dwell within the world then doomed'
 "Must we all hopes of safety then forego?"
"Salvation's road lies open unto all;
 "This is life's way for me—a way of woe!"

XXI

"A way of woe! " These words he scarce had said
   When chilling horror seized the hermit's heart.
Such words betokened bitter discontent—
   How could complaint in his calm life find part?
"A way of woe! " 'Twas cry of suff'ring soul
   Sunk 'neath the load of sadness and distress—
Twas like a sobbing sigh, a mournful moan
   For joy departed and lost happiness . . .
What had he lost? Should he not gladsome feel
   That from the weary world he had withdrawn.
And all its fleeting fancies flung aside
   That for his soul a day of rest might dawn?
It cannot be that still he casts behind
   A longing look on life and its delights,
When upward, e'en to God's most holy throne,
   Sweet immortality his soul invites.
What had come o'er him? What had moved him thus?
   It could not be that now he mourned his fate,
And felt regret that he had yielded all
   To Him, who every being did create!

XXII

He dares not own himself displeased with God;
  The soul that trusts Him He will never leave.
Was not God's blessing generously given?
  He could not wish for more—why did he grieve?
Yea! Yea! His grace was all he could desire . . .
  Then, whence had come those words of deep despair?
Around his cell he glanced, oppressed by fear,
  As if perchance some lurking fiend hid there.
But none was there . . . none save the wearied maid,
  Who, sunk in slumbers soft, in silence lay.
While lovingly on her the firelight glowed
  And flickered o'er her fair face, glad and gay.
Bewitching was she as she lay asleep,
  Adorned in beauty and all charms of love,
As if, seeking to make her fair and good,
  Both love and happiness together strove.
Beauty divine seemed to have shed on her
  All the rich treasures of its boundless store,
And, as the nightingale's upon the rose,
  So beauty's soul upon her cheek did pour.

XXIII

And when the hermit gazed upon that face
  The stormy waves that tossed his heart were still.
Surely some secret force held him enslaved
  That he must look on her against his will!
What power is this that o'er him casts its spell?
  Is it delight, or sorcery's fell snare?
His eyes were traitors to his mind's command;
  He tried to turn away, but still stood there.
Long time he looked . . . then into his cold heart
  At last there streamed a ray, so tender, warm—
He trembled, yet he felt the trembling sweet . . .
  What gave it such a strange and subtle charm?
His agitated heart heaved with quick throbs,
  Ne'er had he felt it thus before this day,
He heard the melody of silver strings;
  As on a lyre, love on his heart did play.
What meant this sweetness hitherto unknown?
  He could not tell this tender feeling's name;
If it was sinful, why was it so like
  Immortal life, his soul's incessant aim?

XXIV

A step he took—himself he knew not why—
  Calm and serene still slept the wearied maid,
And pleasing thoughts pursued her in her dreams,
  While round her parted lips a proud smile played.
And that seducing smile so sweetly lured
  Th' enchanted gazer to a fatal kiss,
None could deny those soul-enticing lips,
  Not e'en an angel fresh from realms of bliss.
Now, lo! the unhappy monk bent down his head
  To kiss her face . . . but seized with swift alarm
He started back . . . 'Twas death's delusive snare
  That sought to draw him by the maiden's charm.
He was not vanquished? Nay, it could not be
  That now his faith had lost its former power—
The thirst for holiness that filled his soul
  Would surely last until life's latest hour!
He could not cast away God's holy gifts,
  The welfare of his soul, and grace divine,
To change them for this earth's harassing cares!
  For passing worldly pleasures dared he pine?

XXV

But who is this that calls reproachfully,
  "Hast thou not fallen into fatal fault!"
Who cries, triumphant o'er his wounded heart:
  "Art thou not vanquished by my first assault?"
Whence comes this sound of noisy, mocking laugh?
  What merriment is this that greets his ear?
No one was there; and yet, it could not be
  That this loud laugh was born of naught but fear I
And tremblingly, with terror, looked he round;
  He was alone . . . still slept the unconscious maid.
In haste he rose, and, filled with wild alarm,
  Before the Holy Virgin bent and prayed.
Is there no help? E'en looking on that face
  The same dismay the hermit's heart assails,
'Gainst that curst laughter, fraught with deep reproach,
  His erstwhile potent prayer naught avails I
His soul entreats his erring heart to pray.
  But all its earnest efforts are in vain;
E'en kneeling 'neath the Virgin's sheltering gaze
  He cannot his rebellious will restrain!

XXVI

He looks upon the holy Virgin's face,
  His supplicating eyes entreat her aid—
But, woe! her gracious smile beams not on him.
  Before him still he sees the shepherd maid.
What brings that form again before his eyes?
  Is it of flesh, or but a phantom pale?
Or has the image of God's Mother changed
  Into the likeness of a mortal frail?
Since he has fall'n, does God not deem him fit
  To look upon the Virgin's holy face?
Has He performed a miracle divine
  To bring His erring servant back to grace?
He tries to cross himself, but lo! his hands
  Refuse to move; he seeks to breathe a prayer,
His tongue is mute; he, thirsting for God's smile,
  Can see naught save the cursed maiden there.
"Now, canst thou still resist?" and in his cell
  The mocking laughter echoed forth once more.
No longer could the unhappy monk remain;
  But, like a madman, rushed forth thro' the door...

XXVII

... The day was dawning, fair the morning broke,
  And from the heav'ns the clouds were chased away,
While o'er the tranquil earth a zephyr breathed
  And everywhere peace held her potent sway ...
But who is this with wildly waving hair
  That runs among the rocks with trembling dread?
It cannot be the monk 1 ... 'Tis he indeed!
  O'er his pale face a death-like hue is spread,
See how he stands upon the very brink.
  And gazes longingly on yonder peaks,
As if he on those lofty mountain heights
  His last and only consolation seeks.
He watches for the sun's first rising ray;
  Why doth it tarry ' Why doth it delay?
Until this day e'en Time itself was naught,
  Why doth a moment now cause him dismay?
—The sun arose! Into his cell in haste
  The monk returned, by dawning hope consoled;
For through his window streamed the sun's
     bright beam.
  And stood there like a pillar, massy gold.

XXVIII

His heart was calmed... Once more with timid trust,
  His eyes he turned towards the Blessed Maid;
Once more the image smiled upon the monk,
  Looking with favour on him as he prayed.
"O God! Thine anger then is turned away!"
  And thankful tears forth from his eyes did well.
He laid his book of prayers upon the ray;
  But, woe! the unhappy man! alas!.. it fell.
Before the hermit's eyes the light grew dim;
  Fear seized his fainting heart, and hopeless dread;
With a wild, wailing shriek of woe he fell,
  In that bright beam, from earth his spirit fled.

* * *

And there where saints once sang there grateful hymns,
  And glorified God's wondrous works and ways,
There where they offered daily sacrifice
  Of lamentation, love, and prayer, and praise,
There, midst the landslips and the broken stones,
  Only the wind moves to and fro, and sighs.
While, fearful of the mighty thunder-clap,
  Within its lonesome lair the wild beast cries.

Tavadi (Prince)
Ilia Chavchavadze
ილია ჭავჭავაძე

ILIA CHAVCHAVADZE: ARCHITECT OF A NATION'S SOUL

To truly comprehend the intricate tapestry of modern Georgia – its fierce pride, its ancient cultural roots, its resilient spirit – one must inevitably encounter the towering figure of Tavadi Ilia Chavchavadze. He is not merely a historical personage or a celebrated author filed neatly away in the annals of literature; rather, he remains a living presence, a foundational intellect whose thoughts and actions continue to shape the contours of Georgian identity. To Georgians, he is quite simply 'Ilia,' a name uttered with a reverence that transcends mere admiration, embodying the very essence of their national awakening in an era of profound challenge and transformation. To speak of Chavchavadze is to speak of the very soul of modern Georgia. He is not merely a writer in the Georgian canon; he is, by almost universal acclaim, its cornerstone, its guiding star, a figure so monumental that his influence resonates through every facet of Georgian national identity even today, well over a century after his death. If Marjory Wardrop was the diligent hand that unlocked a door for us, Ilia Chavchavadze was the master builder who designed and constructed many of the most significant rooms within the house of Georgian consciousness.

Born on 27th October 1837 (by the Julian calendar then in use, which equates to 8th November in the Gregorian calendar) in the village of Kvareli, nestled in the Kakheti region of eastern Georgia – a land renowned for its vineyards and its fiercely independent spirit – Ilia Grigoris dze Chavchavadze was, by birth, a member of the *tavadi*, the Georgian nobility. The Chavchavadze family was an ancient and distinguished one, with a lineage stretching back centuries, deeply entwined with the history and martial traditions of the Kakhetian kingdom. His grandfather had served King Erekle II, a legendary figure in Georgian history. This aristocratic background provided him with a certain standing and, initially, an education befitting his class. However, it also exposed him from a young age to the poignant realities of a proud nation living under foreign dominion. Georgia, having sought Russian protection in the late 18th century, had been progressively annexed by the Russian Empire throughout the early 19th century, its monarchy abolished, its autocephalous Church subordinated, and its native culture increasingly marginalised.

Ilia's early life was marked by tragedy. He lost his mother, Mariam Beburishvili, at a young age, and his father, Grigol Chavchavadze, a man known for his military service in the Russian army but also for his deep Kakhetian roots, passed away when Ilia was still a teenager. These early losses perhaps instilled in him a profound sense of gravity and responsibility. He received his initial education locally, where the seeds of his love for Georgian language and lore were sown, before attending the Tiflis (Tbilisi) Nobility Gymnasium. This was a period of intellectual awakening, but also one where the heavy hand of Russification was increasingly felt in educational institutions.

The truly formative educational experience for Chavchavadze, and indeed for a whole generation of Georgian intellectuals who would later spearhead the national revival, came from his time at the University of St. Petersburg. He enrolled in the Faculty of Law in 1857. St. Petersburg, then the glittering, imposing capital of the Russian Empire, was also a cauldron of intellectual ferment, buzzing with European liberal ideas, debates about social justice, and the first stirrings of revolutionary thought. Here, Chavchavadze encountered the works of Western European thinkers – the Enlightenment philosophers, the Romantic poets, the early socialists – as well as the great Russian writers of the age, such as Pushkin, Lermontov, Gogol, and Belinsky, the latter a particularly influential literary critic and social thinker.

It was in St. Petersburg that Chavchavadze and his fellow Georgian students – men like Akaki Tsereteli, Niko Nikoladze, and Giorgi Tsereteli – formed a loose but immensely influential group known as the *Tergdaleulebi* ("those who have drunk the waters of the Terek"). The Terek River, flowing through the Caucasus mountains, was the symbolic threshold they crossed to gain a Russian education. They returned to Georgia imbued with a potent cocktail of European progressive ideals and a burning, newly sharpened patriotism. Their mission, as they saw it, was to awaken their slumbering nation, to restore its cultural dignity, and to chart a path towards a modern, enlightened future, but one that remained authentically Georgian. Chavchavadze, with his formidable intellect, his commanding presence, and his unwavering commitment, quickly emerged as the natural leader of this movement.

Upon his return to Georgia in 1861, Chavchavadze embarked on a life of relentless, multifaceted activity. He was a poet, a novelist, an essayist, a journalist, a publisher, a banker, a social reformer, and a political activist. It is difficult to overstate the breadth of his endeavours, all driven by a singular, overarching goal: the regeneration of Georgia.

His literary output was both prolific and profound. As a poet, he penned works that ranged from lyrical meditations on nature and love to powerful patriotic odes and philosophical reflections. *The Hermit* (განდეგილი, Gandegili), published in 1883, which is the focus of this volume, is a prime example of his capacity for exploring deep spiritual and existential questions, using the dramatic backdrop of the Caucasus mountains – so integral to the Georgian psyche – as a stage for an internal human drama. Other notable poems include "The Vision" (აჩრდილი, Achrdili), "The Ghost" (მოჩვენება, Mochveneba – though often the same poem as *Achrdili* depending on translation/interpretation), and "The Happy Nation" (ბედნიერი ერი, Bednieri Eri). His poetry often carried a strong national message, lamenting Georgia's past glories, critiquing its present state of apathy or internal division, and inspiring hope for a revived future.

Beyond poetry, Chavchavadze made significant contributions to Georgian prose. His novellas and stories, such as *Kako the Robber* (კაკო ყაჩაღი, Kako Qachaghi), *The Story of a Beggar* (გლახის ნაამბობი, Glakhis Naambobi), *Is a Man a Human Being?!* (კაცია ადამიანი?!, Katsia Adamiani?!), and *Otaraant Widow* (ოთარაანთ ქვრივი, Otaraant Kvrivi), were groundbreaking works of social realism. They painted vivid, often critical, portraits of Georgian society, exposing its flaws – the indolence of some sections of the nobility, the plight of the peasantry, the corrosive effects of ignorance and social injustice. He used satire, pathos, and keen observation to challenge his readers to confront uncomfortable truths about their nation and themselves. These works were not merely literary exercises; they were calls to action, intended to provoke thought and inspire reform.

Perhaps Chavchavadze's most immediate and widespread impact came through his journalistic and publishing activities. In 1863, he founded the journal *Sakartvelos Moambe* (The Georgian Messenger), which, despite its relatively short lifespan due to Tsarist censorship, became a vital platform for the new generation of Georgian intellectuals. Later, and more enduringly, he established the newspaper *Iveria* (Iberia, an ancient name for Georgia) in 1877, which he edited for many years. *Iveria* became the undisputed voice of the Georgian national movement. It published articles on literature, history, economics, education, and current affairs, all aimed at fostering a sense of national unity, promoting the Georgian language, and advocating for social and political progress. Chavchavadze's own essays and editorials in *Iveria* were hugely influential, shaping public opinion and setting the agenda for national discourse.

His famous credo, "Language, Homeland, Faith" (ენა, მამული, სარწმუნოება – Ena, Mamuli, Sartsmunoeba), encapsulated the core tenets of his national vision. He fought tirelessly for the rights of the Georgian language, which was being systematically supplanted by Russian in official life and education. He believed that the language was the lifeblood of the nation, the repository of its culture and identity. "Homeland" signified not just the physical territory of Georgia but also its history, its traditions, and the well-being of its people. He advocated for land reform to alleviate the hardships of the peasantry and sought to modernise the Georgian economy. "Faith" referred to the Georgian Orthodox Church, which had played a central role in preserving Georgian identity throughout centuries of foreign invasions and occupations. Chavchavadze championed the restoration of its autocephaly (independence from the Russian Orthodox Church), which had been abolished by the Tsarist regime.

His practical nation-building efforts were equally remarkable. He was a key figure in the establishment of the Society for the Spreading of Literacy among Georgians (1879), which played a crucial role in promoting education in the Georgian language and publishing affordable books. In a masterstroke of financial acumen and patriotic foresight, he founded the Land Bank of the Nobility in Tbilisi (1875). While ostensibly serving the aristocracy, this bank became a vital financial institution for Georgians of various classes, supporting Georgian enterprise and helping to prevent Georgian lands from falling into the hands of non-Georgian creditors. It was, in effect, a national bank in disguise.

Chavchavadze's path was not without its challenges and controversies. His progressive ideas often brought him into conflict with the more conservative elements of the older generation of Georgian nobility. Later in his life, he also faced criticism from younger, more radical socialist groups who felt his approach was too moderate or too focused on national rather than class struggle. The Tsarist authorities, naturally, viewed his activities with suspicion, and he faced constant censorship and surveillance.

The culmination of these tensions, and a tragic testament to the impact he had, was his assassination. On 28th August 1907 (Julian calendar; 12th September Gregorian), Ilia Chavchavadze, accompanied by his wife Olga Guramishvili, was ambushed and murdered while travelling by carriage from Tbilisi to his estate in Saguramo. The exact motives and the ultimate orchestrators of his assassination remain a subject of debate and speculation to this day. Theories range from involvement by Tsarist secret police seeking to silence a powerful national voice, to radical Bolshevik groups who saw him as an obstacle, to personal vendettas or criminal gangs. What is undisputed is that his death sent a shockwave of grief and outrage across Georgia. His funeral was a massive national event, a testament to the profound love and reverence in which he was held.

The legacy of Ilia Chavchavadze is immeasurable. He is, quite simply, the "Father of the Nation" (ერის მამა – Eris Mama) for Georgians. His writings continue to be read and studied, his ideas debated, and his memory revered. He laid the intellectual, cultural, and to some extent, the institutional foundations for modern Georgian statehood. His tireless advocacy for Georgian language, culture, and self-determination helped to preserve and foster a national identity that would eventually lead to Georgia regaining its independence, first briefly in 1918-1921, and then more enduringly from 1991 onwards.

In 1987, on the 150th anniversary of his birth, Ilia Chavchavadze was canonised by the Georgian Orthodox Church as Saint Ilia the Righteous. This act formally recognised his immense contribution to the spiritual and national life of Georgia, cementing his place not only as a literary and political giant but also as a figure of profound moral and spiritual significance.

When we read *The Hermit*, we are therefore encountering a work by a man whose life was a whirlwind of public action and intellectual engagement, a man who carried the weight of a nation's aspirations on his shoulders. The poem's themes of solitude, spiritual seeking, and the tension between withdrawal from the world and engagement with it, take on a particular resonance when viewed against the backdrop of its author's intensely public and patriotic life. Perhaps it was in such creative explorations of the inner world that Chavchavadze found a necessary counterbalance to the often harsh realities of his political struggles, or perhaps he was subtly exploring different paths to salvation, both for the individual soul and for the soul of his beloved Georgia. Whatever the case, his words, brought to us through Marjory Wardrop's dedicated translation, offer a precious insight into the mind of one of the 19th century's most remarkable nation-builders and literary figures.

MARJORY SCOTT WARDROP: THE INDISPENSABLE INTERMEDIARY

Having now acquainted ourselves with the formidable figure of Ilia Chavchavadze, the poet and patriot who gifted Georgia *The Hermit*, our attention must naturally turn to the remarkable individual whose quiet diligence and profound linguistic gifts first carried his words across the cultural and linguistic chasm to the English-speaking world. For a work so deeply embedded in its native soil, so resonant with Georgian spiritual and national concerns, to find a voice in another tongue requires more than mere technical skill; it demands an intellectual labour of profound empathy, a dedication bordering on the heroic. The name on the spine of that original 1895 English edition, Marjory S. Wardrop, signifies precisely such a monumental effort – the creation of a vital bridge between two disparate literary traditions. Her story, though perhaps lacking the overt swashbuckle of some of her Victorian contemporaries, is one of immense scholarly significance and a testament to the quiet power of cross-cultural understanding, particularly crucial for the appreciation of Georgian literature in the Anglophone sphere.

Right then, let us turn our attention to this remarkable individual whose quiet diligence and profound linguistic gifts first opened the door for English-speaking readers to Ilia Chavchavadze's world: Marjory Scott Wardrop. In the grand, often rather boisterous, theatre of Victorian-era exploration and scholarship, where handlebar moustaches and pronouncements from far-flung corners of the Empire were de rigueur, Marjory Wardrop presents a figure of striking contrast – a woman of gentle determination, immense intellect, and a passion for a culture then largely unknown in the West. Her story is not one of daring escapades in the conventional sense, but of an equally courageous journey into the heart of a complex language and a rich, ancient literary tradition.

Born on 11th November 1869 in Chislehurst, Kent, into a comfortable, educated middle-class family, Marjory grew up in an environment that, while adhering to the societal norms for women of her time, clearly fostered intellectual curiosity. Her father, Thomas Caldwell Wardrop, was a master builder and surveyor, and her mother was Marjory Scott. It was, however, her elder brother, Oliver Wardrop (1864-1948), who would prove to be the pivotal figure in igniting and nurturing her lifelong dedication to Georgia. Oliver, himself a formidable linguist and later a distinguished diplomat – serving as the first British Chief Commissioner of Transcaucasia in Georgia from 1919 to 1921 – was captivated by the languages and cultures of the Caucasus. One can imagine the conversations in the Wardrop household, perhaps Oliver returning from his early travels or studies, regaling his younger sister with tales of this distant, mountainous land, its proud people, and its unique linguistic heritage.

It's crucial to understand the context here. In the late 19th century, Georgia – or *Sakartvelo*, as its people call it – was a relatively obscure corner of the Russian Empire for most Britons. While the "Great Game" played out across Central Asia, and British interests were heavily invested in India and other parts of the Empire, the Caucasus remained somewhat off the beaten track of mainstream British colonial or scholarly focus, though not entirely unknown. For a young woman in Kent to develop an academic obsession with Georgian was, to put it mildly, rather unconventional. The avenues for formal linguistic study for women were limited, and for a language as esoteric (to Western ears) as Georgian, resources would have been exceptionally scarce.

Yet, Marjory Wardrop was undeterred. Possessed of a natural gift for languages – she was reportedly proficient in French, German, Italian, and Russian – she embarked on the formidable task of teaching herself Georgian, most likely with initial guidance and materials provided by Oliver. Georgian, with its unique *Mkhedruli* script and its non-Indo-European grammar, presents a steep learning curve for any Anglophone. The verb system alone is notoriously complex. That she mastered it to the extent she did, largely through self-study, speaks volumes of her intellectual firepower and her unwavering dedication.

Her first published foray into bringing Georgian literature to an English audience was *Georgian Folk Tales*, which appeared in 1894, published by David Nutt in the Strand as part of his "Waifs and Strays of Celtic Tradition" series (an interesting categorisation, hinting at the perceived antiquity and perhaps a certain romantic "otherness" associated with such tales). This was a charming collection, demonstrating not only her linguistic skill but also her ability to capture the narrative voice and cultural nuances of the source material. It was a gentle introduction for British readers to the imaginative world of Georgian folklore.

The following year, 1895, saw the publication by Bernard Quaritch of her translation of Ilia Chavchavadze's *The Hermit* (განდეგილი, Gandegili) – the very work you now hold. This was a more ambitious undertaking. Chavchavadze was, as we've discussed in the general introduction to this volume, a towering figure in contemporary Georgian letters and national life. To tackle one of his significant poetic works required not just linguistic competence but a deep sensitivity to its spiritual and philosophical undercurrents, and an understanding of its place within Georgian culture. Wardrop's translation, rendered in a late Victorian poetic idiom, managed to convey the solemn beauty and gravitas of Chavchavadze's original. It was, for many in Britain, their very first encounter with modern Georgian literature of such artistic merit.

A crucial period in her development as a Kartvelologist (a scholar of Georgian studies) were her visits to Georgia itself. She travelled there in 1894-1895 and again in 1896. These were not casual tourist jaunts. For a single woman to travel to the Caucasus at that time was an adventure in itself, though she was often in the company of her brother Oliver during these expeditions. These journeys allowed her to immerse herself in the language and culture, to interact with Georgian intellectuals, writers, and ordinary people, and to deepen her understanding far beyond what books alone could offer. One can imagine her, diligently taking notes, listening intently, absorbing the atmosphere of Tbilisi (then Tiflis), and perhaps venturing into the countryside that so profoundly shaped Georgian identity. These visits undoubtedly provided invaluable context for her translation work and fuelled her passion further. Contemporary accounts from Georgia, where she is still revered, often speak of her kindness, her genuine interest, and her remarkable linguistic abilities, which impressed her Georgian hosts.

However, the magnum opus with which Marjory Wardrop's name is inextricably linked is her prose translation of Shota Rustaveli's 12th-century epic poem, *The Knight in the Panther's Skin* (ვეფხისტყაოსანი, Vepkhistqaosani). This monumental work is to Georgian literature what Chaucer's *Canterbury Tales* or Dante's *Divine Comedy* are to their respective traditions – a foundational masterpiece, a cultural touchstone. Rustaveli's epic, a complex tapestry of chivalry, romance, friendship, and philosophical wisdom, written in intricate *shairi* quatrains, is notoriously difficult to translate. Many have tried, both before and since, but Wardrop's prose version, published posthumously in 1912 by the Royal Asiatic Society in London, remains a landmark achievement.

She laboured on this immense task for many years, driven by a desire to present Rustaveli's genius to the world in an accessible yet faithful form. Her decision to render it in prose, rather than attempting to replicate Rustaveli's complex poetic structure, was a judicious one. It allowed her to concentrate on conveying the richness of the narrative, the depth of the characters, and the philosophical nuances of the text, without being overly constrained by the demands of English metre and rhyme. Her brother Oliver, in his preface to the 1912 edition, movingly describes her dedication: "Day after day, for hours at a time, she was hunting for the English word or phrase that would justly express the Georgian idea." He speaks of her "unwearied patience" and "minute care."

Tragically, Marjory Wardrop did not live to see this crowning achievement of her scholarly life in print. Her health, never robust, declined, and she passed away on 7th December 1909, in Bucharest, Romania, where Oliver was then serving as British Consul. She was just forty years old. Her death was a profound loss, not only to her family but to the nascent field of Kartvelology in the West.

Oliver Wardrop, devoted to his sister's memory and her scholarly legacy, saw *The Knight in the Panther's Skin* through publication. He also ensured that her valuable collection of Georgian books and manuscripts, painstakingly acquired, found a permanent home. This became the Wardrop Collection at the Bodleian Library, Oxford, which he endowed with the Marjory Wardrop Fund for the encouragement of Georgian studies. This collection, and the fund that supports it, remains a vital resource for scholars to this day, a lasting testament to the siblings' shared passion and Marjory's pioneering efforts. Sir Oliver, in his own right a significant figure in promoting Anglo-Georgian understanding, always ensured his sister's contributions were recognised.

Beyond her major translations, Marjory Wardrop also contributed articles and smaller pieces.

She was a corresponding member of various learned societies and was held in high esteem by the small but growing international community of Kartvelologists. Her work was characterised by its meticulous scholarship, its linguistic precision, and a profound empathy for Georgian culture. She wasn't just translating words; she was translating a worldview, a national spirit.

In assessing her contribution from our 2025 perspective, it's important to acknowledge both the context of her time and the enduring value of her work. Yes, her prose and poetic style are of their era, the late Victorian and Edwardian period. A modern translator might choose different turns of phrase, a more contemporary idiom. But this is to miss the point. Marjory Wardrop was a pioneer. She was venturing into largely uncharted territory, equipped with little more than her intellect, her dedication, and the support of her brother. She built bridges where none existed before. Her translations, particularly of *The Hermit* and *The Knight in the Panther's Skin*, introduced English-speaking readers to masterpieces of a literary tradition that deserved, and still deserves, far wider recognition.

She demonstrated that serious, dedicated scholarship was not the sole preserve of men, even in the more recondite fields of philology. In Georgia, Marjory Wardrop is remembered with immense affection and respect. Streets have been named after her, and her contribution to making Georgian culture known to the wider world is celebrated. She is seen not merely as a translator, but as a true friend of Georgia.

When we read her translation of *The Hermit*, then, we are not just accessing Chavchavadze's poem; we are also encountering the spirit of Marjory Wardrop – her intellectual rigour, her patient dedication, and her profound love for the culture she brought to light. Her life, though tragically short, was one of remarkable achievement, a quiet triumph of scholarship and cross-cultural understanding. She laid a foundation upon which subsequent generations of Kartvelologists in the English-speaking world have been able to build. In the often-overlooked annals of female scholars who expanded the horizons of Western knowledge, Marjory Scott Wardrop deserves a place of particular honour.

WWW.GLAGOSLAV.COM

www.ingramcontent.com/pod-product-compliance
Lightning Source LLC
Chambersburg PA
CBHW061211070526
44583CB00025B/3212